Kayak Touring

Edited by Dave Harrison

Illustrated by Bruce Morser

STACKPOLE BOOKS

Copyright © 1998 by Stackpole Books

Published by
STACKPOLE BOOKS
5067 Ritter Road
Mechanicsburg, PA 17055

Printed in the United States

First edition

10 9 8 7 6 5 4

Cover design by Tracy Patterson

Illustrations © 1990–1997 Bruce Morser. All rights reserved.

The material in this book originally appeared in *Canoe & Kayak* magazine. See page 60 for subscription information.

Library of Congress Cataloging-in-Publication Data

Kayak touring / edited by David F. Harrison—1st ed.
     p.   cm.—(Canoe and kayak techniques)
   ISBN 0-8117-2721-1
   1. Sea kayaking. I. Harrison, David, 1938– . II. Series.
GV788.5.K39 1997
797.1′224—dc21   97-18077
                                        CIP

Contents

Contributors

Dave Harrison is the publisher of *Canoe & Kayak* and author of *Canoeing* (Stackpole Books), and *Sea Kayaking Basics* (Hearst Marine Books).

Shelley Johnson is a sea kayak instructor and co-creator of the video *What Now? Sea Kayak Rescue Techniques*, available at most paddlesports shops.

Lee Moyer operates Pacific Water Sports in Seattle, where he designs and builds sea kayaks and teaches sea kayaking.

David Seidman is the author of *The Essential Sea Kayaker* (International Marine Publishing). He lives on Long Island, New York.

Bruce Morser, a Colgate University graduate who also holds a Master of Fine Arts from the University of Washington, has won many awards for his unique illustrating style. He lives on Vashon Island, Washington.

Introduction

Crossing the North Sea, circumnavigating Iceland, surfing a tidal bore, racing across the Molokai Channel on a pencil-thin kayak: these represent the pinnacle of kayak touring, and there are those who participate at these rarefied levels. There's no reason to set any such lofty goals for yourself at this point; most people will get the greatest satisfaction out of setting attainable and realistic short-term goals and achieving them. That attainment often becomes the new plateau for aiming at a still higher level of proficiency.

Your first task is to assess your own physical and psychic needs. Do you seek high adventure and some risk? Do you tend to "get into" a sport or activity with enthusiasm bordering on obsession? Do you always try to get at the head of the bicycle pace line, reach the summit first, go farther, harder? Trust us, there's a place in kayaking for you.

More folks are likely to be attracted to kayaking as motion pleasure, and a means to see, smell, hear, and be tuned into the natural world. For many, the kayak simply permits them to visit places that can be reached in no other way, to be hunters armed with five senses, or a camera, or binoculars, or a good book. You might also be concerned about the social aspects of the sport: kayak touring as a way to connect with persons sharing a love of the outdoors, or an activity to share with a companion, spouse, or family. No question, this is a lifelong sport.

And there are many kayakers for whom all of the above applies. There's a time for pushing the envelope of adventure and a time to savor the sights, sounds, and sensations. We hope you will find in this book helpful information on building the skills to take you to kayaking at any level that suits you.

The Sea Kayak Launch

Lee Moyer

One nice thing about sea kayaking is that almost anyone can get in and go. But if you overlook some very basic concepts, the get-in-and-go part can be mighty entertaining for spectators.

How do you make your kayak launch go smoothly? Start on shore. Sit in the kayak and adjust the footbraces so they fit snugly. Secure all the gear in and on the kayak. Put on the sprayskirt and lifejacket and have the paddle in hand.

To launch a rigid kayak at a calm beach, put the kayak bow-first in the water at about 45 degrees to the beach and far enough into the water so you can just step into the cockpit from shore. As you step in, the kayak will bottom out; you can sit down, straighten your legs, attach the sprayskirt, and get ready to go while the kayak is aground and stable. Then, turn toward the beach, reach out, place the end of the paddle against the shore, and shove off. Remember, the closer the pushing-off point is to you, the harder it is on you and the paddle (you risk breaking a blade).

In waves, forget the 45-degree angle. Point the kayak directly into the waves hitting the shore. This will prevent the kayak being swept sideways to the beach while you sit down in the water where the kayak was before it moved. Getting all the way into the kayak before it goes sideways isn't much better; the waves break into your lap, and you can't decide whether to put the sprayskirt on as you go firmly aground or to shove off the beach with your paddle as waves keep breaking into your lap.

To launch from a stable platform like a dock or swimming pool edge, you will have to get into a floating kayak. Place the kayak along side the platform with the cockpit next to you. Squat or sit on the platform and place the paddle across from the kayak cockpit's back rim to the platform behind you, like a bridge. With your outboard hand, hold the paddle against the cockpit rim with your thumb around the paddle shaft and fingers in the cockpit. Put your other hand on the shaft on your shore side near where the paddle bears on the platform. Now support your weight on your arms on the paddle shaft. Keeping your weight between your hands, "walk" your legs into the kayak and slide in. Done correctly, this technique puts little stress on the paddle shaft, but a slip can break the shaft. Once you're in, shove away from the platform and attach the sprayskirt.

Carefully consider any launch site. Is there heavy passing traffic? What are the wave patterns? Where will the tide be on your return and what will the beach be like? Since the launch area is usually protected, be sure you know what it will be like out where you are actually going.

90%

45%

In and Out, Gracefully

Shelley Johnson

Visit a busy launch site during peak kayaking season and you'll realize that a surprisingly large number of kayakers do not know how to get in and out of their boats—gracefully, anyway! It is not uncommon to see these sleek and stylish craft repeatedly dump their passengers like a nautical version of a bucking bronco.

Getting in and out of your boat is a matter of balance and support. You must create a support system that anchors all the components to one another: paddler to boat to paddle, and finally to terra firma or whatever else is at hand (dock, ladder, another boat). Some agile youngsters might straddle the boat behind the seat and easily slip in and out, but most of us need a bit more support.

When entering or exiting your boat in calm water, pull parallel to the shoreline or dock. Then take your paddle and place it behind your cockpit coaming—grasping shaft and coaming with one hand—and fully extend the other end of your paddle perpendicular to the kayak. Your paddle becomes an outrigger and support as you slip into or out of your boat, swinging your weight from, or onto, a dock or beach.

To make it all work, several things must occur more or less simultaneously: First, your paddle must remain perpendicular, be fully extended, and be firmly held to the boat for maximum support.

Second, you must enter/exit your boat from the supported side only. Third, the extended paddle must rest on something solid like the shore or dock on the other end. Finally, you need to keep your center of gravity low and your weight only on the side supported by the paddle. Ignoring any of these steps will turn a graceful move into an embarrassing spill.

We've assumed you have access to a conveniently low dock or shallow area for your launchings and landings. If you don't, things can get a bit clumsier, but the same principles hold. If you are entering or exiting your boat in surf, you will need to move quickly to avoid taking on water or having the boat rudely taken from you by a surge. Keep your boat perpendicular to the waves, more out of the water than in it. After you've entered your boat, you can "walk" it to the water with your hands or use your paddle as a push pole. In surf or surge, never exit or enter on the beach side, where you may get clipped by your boat if it is lifted and thrown toward the shore by a wave.

High docks present a real challenge to kayakers. If the top of the dock is reachable from your boat, try hoisting yourself up on your elbows, and then swing your butt up onto the dock, keeping your feet (but very little weight) in your boat. You'll have to give up your paddle for support and, instead, use your arms to support the transfer of weight to the dock.

If you're entering or exiting from a pier with a long drop to the water, you may be forced to use a pier ladder rung as your support system. Again, the trick is to slowly transfer your weight away from your cockpit and onto the ladder. As long as you are firmly anchored to the ladder, the boat should remain in place and be a reasonably stable platform. Once you're out of the boat, a line can be attached to the ladder to temporarily hold the boat.

No matter what situation you find yourself in, you should always employ the same principles. Keep your center of gravity low and your weight to the supported side. Make sure the support system is solid, the paddle shaft held to your boat on one end, with the extended end resting on a secure platform—shore, dock, pier, or ladder.

Use your paddle as outrigger and support.

Be at One with Your Kayak

David Seidman

A kayak isn't like a car. You can't just get in, adjust the seat, and go. A kayak must be custom fitted to your body, so the boat makes solid contact with your feet, knees, hips, rear, and back. The fit should be snug enough so that you "lock in" when you flex your feet and thighs—so you're at one with the kayak. Only then can you paddle with control and comfort.

However, manufacturers build their kayaks to accommodate as wide a variety of body types as possible. Like a suit or dress bought off the rack, it is the rare boat that provides a perfect fit. Some alterations are almost always necessary.

If you can't bring yourself to shave some foam or otherwise modify what took two years to save for, your dealer can do the work for you. But don't be afraid to do it yourself. You'll need some MiniCel (closed-cell) foam, a knife, hacksaw, sandpaper, and adhesive. For fiberglass boats, a waterproof marine contact cement like Sea Bond is fine; plastic boats may require special adhesives—ask what the manufacturer or dealer recommends.

When you've assembled your materials, concentrate on these five critical points of contact:

FEET

The balls of your feet transmit the forward forces from the paddle and your body to the kayak. Adjust the foot pedals or bar so that your knees touch the underside of the deck and your lower back (from the waist down) gently presses into the back of the seat. Your heels should be close together, toes turned slightly outward, and feet at not quite 90 degrees to your ankles.

KNEES

Balancing and leaning forces are directed through the knees. The farther apart they are (without being uncomfortable), the better your side-to-side balancing will be. They should just touch the underside of the deck near the sides of the boat. Cushion this area with padding; if your knees do not make contact, build up layers of foam to fill the space. Some boats let you brace the upper part of your thighs against the coaming. These areas may also need padding.

HIPS

Your hips help control and balance the boat. If needed, place foam blocks between your hips and the side of the boat. Don't pack yourself in so tightly that you have trouble getting in or out, or that an extra layer of clothing will affect the fit. Leave about a half-inch on either side.

REAR

Your seat should be as low as possible to gain stability, but not so low that it will hinder your stroke. It should provide friction to keep you from sliding around (try lining your seat with a thin layer of foam), and be sloped at the same angle as your thighs for support.

BACK

Both the seat and the back support help lock you in and transmit the paddle and body forces that stop, slow, or reverse the boat. The back support should be no higher than necessary—the backrest is not there for your relaxation. If yours extends too high up, it will restrict your body motion and should be lowered.

If you can achieve a snug fit at these five points of contact, you'll be more comfortable and paddle more efficiently, since the forces generated by the paddle can pass through your body and to the boat more directly.

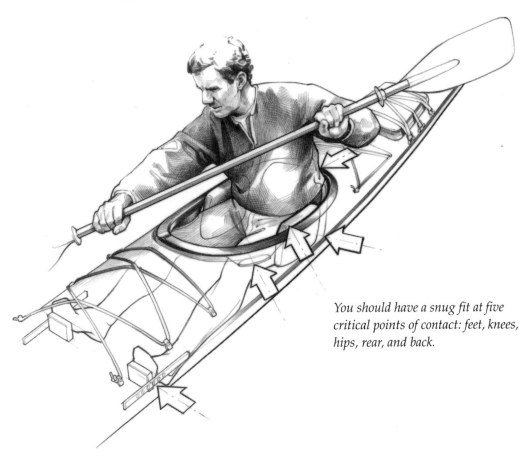

You should have a snug fit at five critical points of contact: feet, knees, hips, rear, and back.

The Key to Paddling Forward? Relax

Lee Moyer

Compared to other paddlers, the sea kayaker does almost nothing but paddle forward. Where a river paddler uses the current and a few very stressful strokes here and there to maneuver, the sea kayaker performs ten thousand strokes in a day, each one just slightly stressful. The most natural stroke for even a rank beginner is still the one that needs the most refinement.

Position your hands so that as you touch the paddle shaft to your chest, your hands are just outside your shoulders. Your grip should be just strong enough to hold the paddle in control. On the push part of the stroke your hand should be open, like you had just released a shot put. The shaft extends under your partially extended fingertips and is supported on the inside of your thumb. This angling of the shaft under your fingers allows you to keep your hand and fingers aligned with your forearm and not bent side to side. This reduces forearm stress. To pull, close just your forefinger around the shaft. To keep your hands relaxed, it helps to think of keeping your hands open to dry them.

Most of the power comes from your torso rotation, not your arms. For the catch, rotate your shoulders to face the opposite side, extend your lower arm fully, and place the blade in the water close to the bow as far forward as you can reach. Punch your upper arm straight ahead at the horizon, rotate your torso, and push with your paddling-side foot while you allow your lower arm to drop and swing out. Complete the stroke by continuing to pull with your torso and lower arm, bending it at the elbow to retrieve the paddle from the water. As your hand gets near your shoulder, you are set up for the stroke on the opposite side.

Practice to make the stroke smooth and relaxed. The stroke is impossible without well-fitted footbraces, knee-thigh support, and seat; you should be sitting up like your mother used to tell you, with comfortable lower back support. Your head should stay in one place relative to the kayak while your torso and shoulders rotate. The center of the paddle can move side to side somewhat, but it should stay low. Keep your upper hand below the horizon.

As your lower hand reaches your hip, the power phase is complete and your blade should leave the water quietly. The elbow bends at this point as you set up for the opposite stroke. Good forward strokes are silent, so experiment with the timing of your pull and recovery, the angle of the blade on entry and exit, your grip, and even seemingly unrelated things like footbrace adjustment.

In wind you will have to grip the paddle tighter and use a flatter stroke. Drop into low gear by sliding your hands farther apart and taking shorter strokes close to the bow. A smooth forward stroke takes concentration at first, but with practice it will become natural and subconscious.

Most of your power comes from your torso, not your arms. Your torso should rotate enough so that your PFD zipper moves side to side. Note the open hand during forward thrust.

It's All in the Grip

David Seidman

Unlike our whitewater cousins, who depend on the river, we have to paddle to get where we're going. Ninety percent of what we do is straight paddling, with an occasional brace thrown in for excitement. And if you're going to do that much of anything, you'd better master the fine points. You will want to develop a style of your own, one that is efficient enough to carry you long distances and comfortable enough to be maintained for hours. As your style evolves you have to make choices, and one of the most important is how you hold the paddle.

Your hand position on the shaft will be determined by your stroke. And, since

Slide your hands out for grunt paddling against the wind or when you need a burst of acceleration. Shift to a narrower grip for higher RPM paddling while cruising in calmer conditions.

your stroke will vary, so will the position of your hands. For maximum power to accelerate, maneuver, or push into a current or headwind, use a wide grip. This is like low gear on a car, giving a slower but more powerful stroke. If you bring your hands closer together, you get a higher gearing, with more blade action in proportion to arm movement. Your high gear is used to sustain a cruising speed, or for faster traveling in calm conditions.

To effectively shift gears you have to know the range of hand positions. The outer limits of your grip are determined by holding the paddle over your head. Make a right angle with your elbows so your forearms are vertical and upper arms horizontal. This is the position for maximum low gear. Mark the shaft with tape just outside of your little fingers, making sure that the marks are equal distances from the center. To find the limit for high gear, bring the shaft up to your shoulders with arms against your side. Mark the shaft near your thumbs. Your effective range is between those marks.

How the paddle is gripped depends upon which hand you choose to be your control hand. This hand holds the shaft so that the top edge of the blade lines up with the top row of your knuckles. Maintain that grip so you'll always know the angle of the blade in relation to your hand. Blade angle in relation to the water is changed by moving your wrists or forearms, not by loosening your grip and turning the shaft. Once you change your grip you lose your orientation to the blade, making the blade's angle a constant guessing game and quick response bracing an impossibility.

But don't keep a death-grip on the shaft either. The pulling hand holds the shaft in the curve of your fingers with most of the gripping done by the thumb and forefinger. Keep a light and responsive hold. It may seem too delicate, but your fingers will close automatically when needed, so don't worry. The pushing hand's fingers are kept slightly open, with the palm and the webbing between thumb and forefinger taking most of the pressure. By keeping a relaxed grip on both hands, you get a longer stroke and reduce lateral wrist movements that can stress tendons.

Finding Your Forward Stroke

Shelley Johnson

Everyone at sometime in his or her paddling life has probably had an instructor or paddling buddy point out the incredible virtues of torso rotation. Rather than belabor that point here, let's look at how you can develop and easily maintain a forward stroke that is efficient and comfortable for you. Understanding where the tradeoffs are between being a techniques snob and a relaxed Sunday driver will mean that when you choose, you can trot out your best forward stroke to wow the crowds or, conversely, know what you're giving up in power and efficiency when you choose to be a techniques slob. It's all a matter of style!

Power in the forward stroke does indeed come from torso rotation. How do you check yourself for torso rotation? First, check what your shoulders are doing on each stroke. If they are squared with the boat, instead of leading with the paddle placement of each stroke on that side, you probably aren't rotating. You should see the life vest zipper moving side to side as you complete your forward stroke. Think of having a bell attached to your bellybutton; it should ring with each stroke!

Another good way to check your torso rotation is to take a few strokes with your elbows locked straight. With both elbows locked through several strokes you'll find that you must rotate your torso to take a stroke. If this motion feels completely bizarre, you probably haven't been rotating your torso prior to this test. Gradually ease off of the locked elbows but don't let your lower arm bend too much or you'll get into the habit of powering your strokes with a pulling motion which uses the weaker muscles of your upper arms rather than the longer, more powerful muscles of your back and torso. Also, try watching your paddle blade from catch to finish with each stroke. This isn't a great way to see and enjoy the seascape, but it will help induce torso rotation.

Watch your upper hand as it moves forward on the pushing part of your stroke. If you can't see it, it's too high. The upper hand should be at a comfortable height, no higher than your nose for an easy touring stroke. Anything higher is either a power stroke or a shoulder problem waiting to happen. Envision having a mirror mounted on the bow of your boat. With every stroke, that upper hand should punch your image on the chin. But remember to keep an easy, delicate grip on the paddle to avoid wrist and forearm fatigue and protect the wrist from repetitive motion problems.

Don't forget your lower body. Your stroke starts from your feet as they gently push on the foot pegs with each stroke. An easy touring stroke doesn't warrant a lot of leg action, but you can crank it up a notch by driving the stroke a bit more from your legs. If your boat begins bobbing with each stroke, you've definitely overdone it! Remember, we are discussing a touring stroke whose rhythm should allow you to paddle for hours with ease, not a powerful racing stroke.

Now it's time to sit up straight, put your forward stroke together, and smooth out the rough spots. Get used to checking your stroke as you paddle until your forward stroke reaches an easy and comfortable rhythm. There is no right or wrong forward stroke. Instead, there are forward strokes that waste a lot of your energy and limit how far and where you can go, and there are forward strokes that are smooth and easy all day long. Understanding the tradeoffs and knowing how to check yourself as you paddle will allow you to make your own choices and paddle with your own style.

Where are your shoulders, elbows, hands, and feet?

Push While You Pull

David Seidman

Most of the power in your forward stroke should come from the twisting of your torso, a little less from the pulling arm, and the rest from a pushing force by the non-pulling arm. By adding this extra pushing power, you'll immediately find a great strain has been taken off your pulling wrist and that paddling has become a lot easier than it used to be.

The additional pushing motion is like using two hands to turn a steering wheel rather than one. Or, if you prefer a more literal image, it might help to think of the paddle as a lever.

Envision that at the start of each stroke the blade is being inserted into something solid and you are pulling the boat toward it. With this action you are using the paddle as a lever. Unfortunately it is a very inefficient one, but with the addition of some pushing from the non-pulling arm we can improve this markedly.

This time envision a new and more complex lever. Like all levers, it needs a pivot point, a fulcrum—your pulling hand. As before, you are trying to move an immovable blade through the water to pry the boat forward. But now, the motive forces will come from both the pulling and pushing arms.

What makes this lever complex is that your pulling hand becomes a movable fulcrum. As it hauls the boat toward the blade, it is also acting as a pivot point for the shaft, which is being pushed forward by the higher, non-pulling arm. The result is a combined increase in power from the hauling of the pulling arm, and leveraged prying of the pushing arm.

However you understand it, both arms are now sharing the work. The balance isn't even, with about 65 percent of the force coming from the pulling and 35 percent from the pushing, but it is more than enough for you to be able to notice a tremendous difference in performance.

The pushing begins as soon as you start the stroke, with the two arms moving in opposite directions and at similar speeds. The pushing force increases through the middle of the stroke, around where your knee passes the blade. At this point both arms are equally extended and maximum pushing power is being applied. The arms continue with reduced force until the lower blade is at the end of its stroke, and the upper pushing arm almost at the limit of its reach. The total motion of the pushing arm is like a slow forward punch coming from your shoulder toward the centerline at the bow.

There is a tendency to get over-enthusiastic about pushing. Some paddlers may complete the push way before the pull is finished, or may apply maximum push before the pull has even started. While learning, keep your pace down, using gentle pressure so you can feel the pushing and pulling, and where the two change places.

Do not bring the pushing hand above eye level, drop it near the end of the stroke, cross the boat's centerline, or hold the shaft too close to your chest. And don't develop a death grip with the pushing hand. Keep fingers relaxed and slightly open with the palm taking most of the pressure.

Cruising Speed

Shelley Johnson

Whether you're planning an afternoon paddle or a multi-day expedition, it is essential to know how fast you paddle, or stated another way, how far you can paddle in a given period of time. Even though your speed can be affected by wind, tidal currents, or even boat traffic, knowing your average cruising speed will make trip planning more meaningful and give you a basis for determining the effects of other factors on you and your boat.

Speed is always a measure of distance over time. Since you'll want to use your known cruising speed to plan trips, using nautical charts, you should show your speed in knots, or nautical miles per hour. A nautical mile is slightly longer than a statute mile. Distances in nautical miles are easily determined when working off a nautical chart since one minute of latitude also gives you a measure of one nautical mile. Minutes of latitude (sixty minutes equals one degree) are shown as hash marks on the edges of charts, so you can use this handy reference to determine how far you have paddled or would like to paddle.

There are several ways to determine your cruising speed, which we'll define as the normal speed you can easily maintain over the course of a day's paddle. Obviously, your sprint speed will be significantly faster than your "stop and look at everything" speed.

Many charts will show an area that has a measured nautical mile clearly noted on either end by a buoy or other marker. If you're lucky enough to find one of these in your paddling area, use it to determine your cruising speed. You can also mark off your own course and then time yourself over at least a nautical mile. David Burch, in his book *Kayak Navigation*, points out that a boat seventeen feet long that passes a stationary mark in five seconds is traveling at about two knots. You can put this useful conversion to work in determining the speed of a current you may have encountered or to quickly get an estimate of your own paddling speed.

You'll probably find that your average cruising speed falls somewhere between 2.0 and 4.0 knots. Once you've determined your average cruising speed, then you can begin some accurate trip planning. For example, on a planned trip of six nautical miles at a cruising speed of three knots you can expect to arrive at your destination in two hours. Knowing this single fact will allow you to determine just what might affect your speed and why. Try to break your trip into segments with individual estimates of arrival time at each site to gain a greater understanding of your actual speed. For instance, note your estimated time from your launch site to a rest stop, and then from there to your lunch spot.

A known cruising speed is the basis for most of your navigation and certainly all of your trip planning. Since it's your trip, it should be your cruising speed that is factored in, not some other paddler's. So get out and determine your cruising speed and how it is influenced by wind and current. Then you can have fun refining your trip planning and navigation skills. It could mean the difference between a good outing and a long, miserable day.

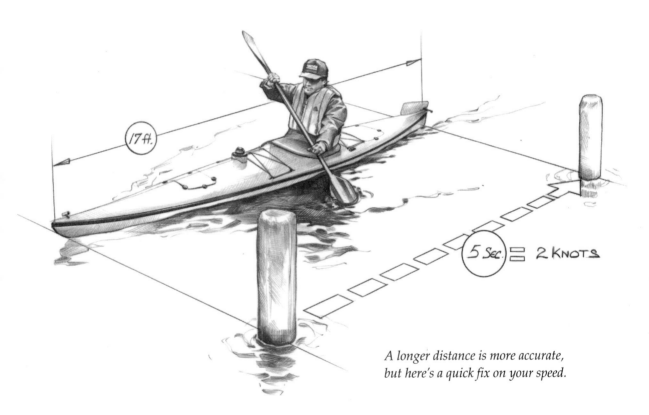

A longer distance is more accurate, but here's a quick fix on your speed.

Paddling in Following Seas

Shelley Johnson

Paddling in following seas can be either a lot of fun or a real chore, depending on your timing and frame of mind. Having a wave grab you from behind and lift your stern can be a bit disconcerting, especially to the novice kayaker. Relax, keep your boat headed down the wave, and enjoy the free ride!

Use the wave's energy to your advantage: paddle hard to catch the wave and pick up speed, then slide down its face. As the wave passes under you, you'll find yourself in the trough with the backside of that wave in front of your boat. Relax at this point. There's no sense in wasting a lot of energy trying to paddle uphill. Slow your paddling cadence down, make sure you're positioned to take advantage of the next wave, and wait for it to give you a lift. If the wave isn't very steep, lean forward a bit as you paddle down the wave to take full advantage of the downhill momentum. If the wave is steeper, you might have to lean back to avoid burying the bow of your boat (pearling) as you gain speed down the face of the wave.

As your boat's stern is lifted, your bow will have a tendency to swing to one

The crux moment at the crest of the wave. Even a rudder loses its effectiveness.

side or the other; if uncorrected, your boat will broach, or in other words, be caught sideways to the wave. The earlier you catch this swing, the easier it is to bring your boat back on track. You can keep your boat pointing down the face of the wave by using your paddle to draw or pry your stern back into the wave as needed. This will keep your boat headed down the wave face and not waste your momentum by moving side to side. As you get used to this tendency, you'll have your paddle ready for a quick maneuver to bring your boat back on track when needed.

If you do broach on the wave, make sure to lift the lower side of your boat as you slide down the wave. By leaning your boat into the wave you'll avoid catching the lower edge and flipping. Be ready with a bracing or support stroke on the top of the wave if needed. Lean into this brace and keep your elbows in close to your body to protect your shoulder joint. As the crest of the wave moves under you, make a strong sweep (or reverse sweep) stroke and bring the boat back perpendicular to the wave. It's easier to turn your boat on the crest of the wave than at any other point because less of your boat is in the water.

Depending on the type of boat you paddle, you might find a rudder system to be a real advantage. It does increase drag, but if your boat has much rocker or you are heavily loaded, dropping the rudder might be the way to go. If your boat tends to track well, forget the rudder and just have your paddle ready for a quick correction when needed.

If you don't mind elevator rides, paddling in following seas can be enjoyable and a quick way to travel. However, if you fight for control and to maintain a single rhythm to your paddling, you might be in for a long day. Paddling on open water and adjusting to existing sea conditions are part of the fun and challenge of sea kayaking. But it's only fun when you understand what is happening to your boat and what techniques to use under variable conditions. Instead of fighting the conditions, look for a pattern and paddle within its constraints. Don't sweat the small stuff; save your energy for the big stuff out there!

Hula Hips:
Responding to Wave Action

Dave Harrison

Hawaiian paddlers are fond of sit-on-top kayaks called surf skis, with long, skinny hulls that the uninitiated find tippy in the extreme. Yet, they paddle in the open ocean, often in huge seas, or along coastlines where ocean swells reflect off of sheer lava cliffs. In other words, they know how to deal with rough water. Hawaiian paddlers have a great term for tipping over, "huli," which means to be turned (as on a spit). It stands to reason, therefore (even if the taxonomy is flawed), that the antidote to a "huli" is to learn to roll the hips, as in the Hawaiian dance, the hula.

On a recent outing closer to home, as we prepared to return across a channel which was beginning to show whitecaps, one of our group asked if he should lean into the big waves which would surely be coming at his beam. I suggested, rather, that he roll his hips to keep the boat level with the horizon, no matter what the waves were doing. The common reaction of inexperienced and anxious paddlers to increasing wave action is to lock up the hips. With the hips locked (usually accompanied by hard pushing on the foot pedals or pegs), the kayak and occupant become fused into a top-heavy "Bongo Boy," pitching with the waves and threatening to capsize.

Think of your relationship to the boat and the waves as being like a yacht's gimbal—you know, the suspension system for the compass (or a cocktail) that keeps it level even as the yacht tosses from side to side. Hula hips are your own gyroscopic adjustment system, whereby you roll your hips to keep the boat level no matter where it sits on the plane of a wave—its top, its back, or its face. In fact, kayakers have a unique ability to remain upright, even stable, in enormous seas that would have most yachtsmen at wit's end. As a kayaker, you enjoy two critical attributes that make this so: Your center of gravity is below the waterline, and unlike the yachtsman, you can, by using your hula hips, adjust the boat's relationship to the wave face(s).

Fortunately, learning to use hula hips is a lot easier than learning the hula. Also, most of you won't have to learn it on one of those pencil-thin surf skis. A simple drill, and one which also sets the stage for learning the low brace, should be part of a warm-up routine you do every time you get on the water in your kayak. A snugly (not tightly) fitted seat and the hip clips make this an even more rewarding exercise. Sit in your kayak on quiet water, sprayskirt on, and paddle in a relaxed position in front of you. Hip action is really knee action, and that's exactly how you will get your hula into motion. Slowly lift your left knee (relaxing the other) to cock your boat to the right. Keep your body centered over the mid-line of the kayak; only the boat leans, not you. Try to cock your boat right over on its right edge. At the moment of imminent capsize (in your mind, at least), quickly bring up the right knee and drop the left knee. Now repeat to the other side. You may find that you can ignore this sequence and simply begin rocking your boat side to side using your knees and hips. Cock the boat back and forth slowly; then do it rapidly. See how far on edge you can get the boat.

What many folks refer to as a "sense of balance" is nothing more than a subconscious adjustment to an unstable environment, in the sea kayaker's case, waves and swell. The simple drill described above needs to be programmed into muscle memory to serve as your gyroscope when the seas begin to move. Remember: keep your body over the centerline of the boat. Relax, think low, and let your hula hips roll with the ocean's punch.

Use hip and knee action to keep a level kayak on any face of the wave.

The Draw Stroke

Dave Harrison

One of the problems with the modern touring kayak—especially one with a rudder—is that it's too easy to make it go somewhere. Lots of people go somewhere in their kayaks before they learn how to control the boat in other than ideal conditions. If you never plan to leave unprotected waters, that's probably OK. Among newcomers to the sport, there seems to be an inordinate fascination with the Eskimo roll; the truth is, you should never need a roll if you have mastered all of the paddle strokes and braces which give you control over your boat.

One of those strokes is the draw stroke. For whitewater paddlers, it is an essential river running tool. For sea kayakers, its principal application may be for sidling up to a dock, but you want to learn the draw stroke for other reasons. When you master the draw stroke, you have mastered blade control; ultimately, blade control equals boat control. A properly executed draw stroke also demands extreme torso rotation, an important—but often missing—component of virtually every other kayak stroke.

First, what does the draw stroke do? At the most basic level, it moves the boat sideways. Whitewater kayaks tend to have a flat bottom, and the ends of the boat are out of the water, so they can be pulled sideways with relative ease. But going sideways is a fair challenge in a boat that is designed to go mainly in a straight line.

Learn the draw stroke on flat, calm water. Your objective is to see how far, and with how few strokes, you can move the boat laterally, in each direction. To execute the draw, hold your paddle out in front of you, elbows straight, and rotate your torso (at the waist, not just the shoulders) so that you and your PFD zipper are aimed in the direction you want to go. As you rotate, move your forearm and top hand across your forehead; the top hand should extend over the water. Plant the blade with the paddle shaft vertical, and the blade as far from the boat as possible. Now, pull the boat to the blade and get the blade out of the water before it goes under the boat. Replant the blade and repeat the draw stroke until you have moved the boat, say, 10 feet in one direction; make the same move on the other side. If you don't rotate your body sufficiently, you'll have a tough time getting that top hand out over the water. The paddle shaft will not be vertical and you'll be pushing water down with your blade instead of pulling the boat to the blade.

After you have accomplished a few good sideways moves by doing successive draw strokes, try the sculling draw. This gives you very precise control over your lateral movement. With the blade planted 90 degrees away from the cockpit, carve a figure 8 with your paddle blade, using blade angle changes to create pressure and a side-slip of the hull. The sensation is much like the lift created (every kid has done this) when you hold your flat hand out of a moving car window and make subtle changes in the plane of your hand. Sculling with your blade allows you to keep slicing the blade away from the hull, and you can side slip indefinitely without taking your paddle out of the water.

The reality in most cruising situations is that you may only have occasion to move your boat sideways for a few moments out of a whole day of paddling. If it happens to be the necessary move in a rescue situation, you might take a different view of the draw stroke's utility value. Therefore, the greatest value in practicing and mastering the draw stroke—especially the sculling draw—is that it teaches you blade "feel" and blade control; that is, where is your paddle blade in relation to your boat, your body, and your paddle shaft? What subtle changes in arm, wrist, and body position are required to make the paddle blade do what you want it to do?

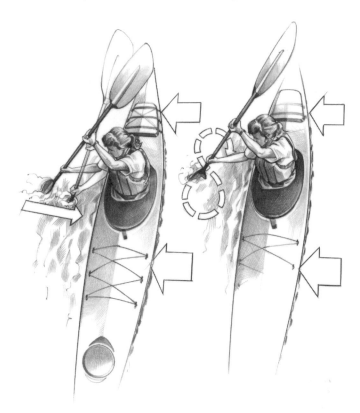

Turn the Other Cheek (and Other Tips for Turning)

Lee Moyer

Making a kayak turn adequately is so easy it needs no explanation of the obvious, but turning efficiently and smoothly takes technique and body control. The specific turning technique you need depends on your desired rate of turn, whether it's for a mere course correction or a quick pivot on the crest of a wave.

For a minor course correction, or to simply allow for a kayak's tendency to turn to one side, continue to paddle ahead smoothly but go deeper on one side and wider on the other. To veer left, for example, paddle deep and close to the kayak on the left and wide and shallow on the right.

To increase the rate of turn, turn the other cheek. That is, lift your inside knee and lean your butt into the outside of the turn. This makes the hull much more responsive to the turning stroke. Once you start your turn with the uneven paddle stroke, straight paddling with a lean will continue the turn. As you approach your desired heading, level the kayak to stop the turn.

You can add even more correction by incorporating a sweep stroke on the right rather than a wide forward stroke. (Yes, there is a difference between a sweep and a wide forward stroke.) To sweep, roll your wrists slightly forward and as you start the stroke, pull out of the side with your lower hand before you start to push your upper hand forward and rotate your shoulders. The idea is to get the blade angled so it pushes sideways on the water as if you were planting the paddle and rotating your feet away from it. In a forward stroke, you plant the paddle and pull back on the water, even in a wide, turning forward stroke. In a single kayak, the entire sweep stroke is a turning stroke and the follow-through is effective until it touches the back of the kayak. In a double kayak, only the first half of the sweep in the bow and the last half of the sweep in the stern are effective. In synchronized forward paddling, each paddler of a double does an abbreviated sweep on the outside of the turn and an easy deep forward stroke on the inside.

The next improvement is to turn the kayak while it is on the crest of a wave rather than in a trough. With the kayak's ends mostly out of the water and its center supported on the wave, the kayak turns more responsively. Skiers call it turning on a mogul.

By incorporating a subtle combination of asymmetric paddling, the sweep stroke, leaning the hull, and timing your turn with the waves, you gain very effective control of your kayak with little effort while you appear to do nothing but paddle straight ahead. The secret is not to overcorrect.

One Good Turn: The Sweep Stroke

Dave Harrison

You spend most of your time in a sea kayak going in a straight line, but you need some turning strokes in your repertoire if you really want to be in control in a variety of situations.

Whether you need to navigate a tight spot as you attempt to exit the marina, or you need to make a sharp correction in rough water to get your kayak pointed in the right direction, a sweep stroke is often the answer. You might even need a quick sweep stroke to keep you going in a straight line.

"What's wrong with a hard rudder right—or left," you might ask. Well, some kayaks don't have rudders, and yours

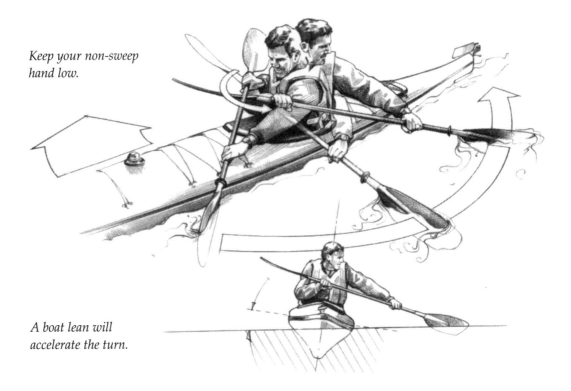

Keep your non-sweep hand low.

A boat lean will accelerate the turn.

might become disabled; it happens. Moreover, the radius of a rudder-driven turn may not be sufficient, or you may need action fast! A sweep, in addition to a rudder, can accelerate your turn and tighten your radius.

A sweep is executed on the side you are turning away from. In the forward stroke the paddle blade moves parallel to the keel line; for the sweep, you carve an arc with your blade.

Start the sweep by planting the blade as far forward as possible and push the blade outward, sweeping it in a broad arc, and finishing with a powerful draw of the blade toward the stern of the boat. Your non-sweeping, or inside, hand stays low, moving across the deck in front of you, rather than punching out in front of you as it does in the forward stroke. Blade orientation is important for the sweep. Twist the blade by rolling your wrist forward slightly so that the blade will sweep water away from the bow.

Since most of the turning impetus occurs at the start and the end of the stroke, you will eventually learn to dispense with a full sweep. If you simply twist your body toward the rear of the kayak and plant your paddle blade at the halfway point in the arc between cockpit and stern and draw the stern toward the paddle, you will have a stroke that, in fact, has a name: the stern draw.

Torso rotation is very important. In practicing the stroke, keep your eye on the sweeping blade throughout the arc; this forces your shoulders and torso to follow.

It may take several sweeps, or stern draws, to turn the boat, and even this may not get you turned as fast as you'd like. Here's another trick to accelerate the turn. As you stroke, cock the boat over on its edge, toward the outside of the turn. That gets the ends of the boat out of the water and creates a "rockered" bottom that turns rather than tracks.

Practice your sweep stroke—and work on cocking or leaning your boat too—on flat water, and see how sharp a radius you can achieve. Out on real water, you'll have one more weapon in your arsenal for slaying the control dragon.

Rudders and Skegs

Lee Moyer

Rudders and skegs are devices to aid in the control of a sea kayak, primarily as trim devices to improve tracking, often in the wind. Without getting into the pros and cons of rudders and skegs, most would agree that, like other equipment, there are techniques for using them well. The point is to understand what they do; used improperly, they can be dangerous.

Rudders are foot-controlled, steerable fins installed on the back end of a kayak. Virtually all rudders are retractable by the paddler and kick up automatically when they hit something. A rudder will make any kayak design work well in the wind, and it is a good way to compensate for a lightly loaded or improperly trimmed kayak, or a design that is

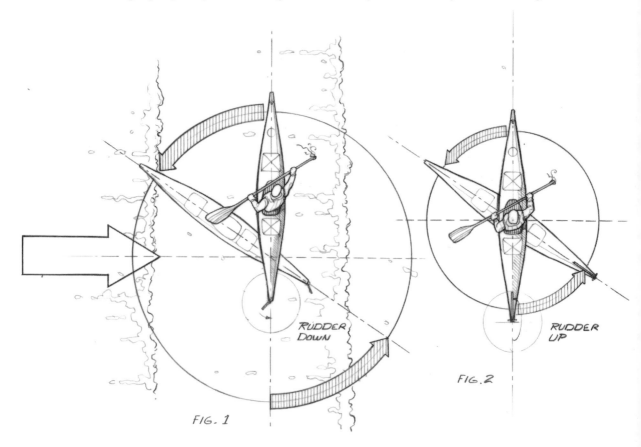

FIG. 1

FIG. 2

not well balanced in the first place. It saves work and sometimes is a way to help a weaker paddler.

The rudder can help you control your path in wind and waves. If conditions are such that the kayak is difficult to turn into the wind—say, due to steep waves—paddle hard and build up speed before you try your turn. Then use strong forward sweeps to maintain speed and help the turn while you use the rudder. The turn will be slow, and actual turning may occur only during one phase of the waves. Don't give up: you may have to maintain the effort during several waves before you can see that the turn is working.

To use the rudder, one must maintain forward paddling speed so the rudder blade can react against the flow of water. Forward sweep strokes and a touch of rudder will aid a broad turn, but in tight quarters a rudder actually inhibits maneuverability (see figure 2). A sharp turn requires a reverse sweep. A rudder is designed to resist this. Retracting the rudder will make your job easier.

Skegs are retractable, non-steerable fins attached to the back of the kayak or the bottom of the hull near the stern. They aid in tracking, inhibit turning, and can be dangerous in wind if they cannot be retracted or if you don't understand how they work. By adding a skeg, a kayak that tracks poorly will track well in calm conditions. Thus, many paddlers new to using skegs do fine until they are in a downwind situation and find they can't turn around. Since the skeg helped before, often it doesn't occur to them to retract it. In fact, the skeg may make it *impossible* to turn into the wind since the paddler has to rotate the whole kayak around by pivoting on the stern, which is anchored by the skeg, up into the wind. Sweep strokes turn the kayak around its center and work poorly to turn the kayak around its end. With the skeg retracted, the stern can slip downwind, and the kayak can pivot from amidships.

The obvious caveat is "what if it fails?" Rudders and skegs usually are reliable. But only a fool would bet his life against one never failing.

Build Confidence with Braces

Lee Moyer

The object of a brace is to help you stay upright when you're falling over. And, of course, since a brace will help you recover from an unstable position, it is a boon to your confidence when the going gets rough.

During a brace, you push or pull on the water with the flat of the paddle blade and use your hips and legs to pull the kayak back under you. The pushing brace is called the low brace. To recover from an imminent flip with the low brace, you quickly push (or slap) at the water with the back (non-power face) of the blade and snap your hips to move the kayak back under you. Your paddle shaft is below your elbows the entire time. The pulling brace, or high brace, differs from the low brace in two ways: it uses the power face of the blade and requires that the paddle shaft be above your elbows. For either brace, all of the paddle control is obtained by rotating your wrists and elbows and even "unwinding" your grip, but your grip never changes from the basic forward paddling position.

There are two parts to any brace: body action and paddle action. The key to proper body action is understanding that you do not brace to push yourself back up onto the kayak but to stop your fall while you pull the kayak back under you with your legs and hips.

To feel the difference, sit in your kayak, hold onto the side of a pool, dock, or a friend's hands, and tip over the boat till your head is just above the water, your body is in the water, and the kayak has flipped overcenter (it wants to turn completely upside down). Now try to right yourself. It's hard work because you are trying to keep your head up and out of the water and are lifting your whole body out of the water as it extends away from the kayak.

Now, try it again. Tip the boat over, but this time keep your head in the water, lean forward to keep your body under water and close to the kayak, and quickly pull your lower knee toward your lower elbow to bring the kayak under you. Once the boat is under you, then bring your torso and finally your head out of the water. Remember, your head comes up last. "Bend at the waist," "flip your hips," "keep your head down," and "pull your knee under you" are all phrases instructors use to describe this easy body action. When you get it, you'll be surprised at how little effort is actually required.

So while you're using your body to right yourself, what do you do with your paddle? Start the low brace by holding the paddle low and close to your stomach, your elbows high, and your wrists rotated forward so the back of the blade is flat and just above the water. Without tipping the kayak, extend the paddle as far out to the side as possible. Slowly start to lean toward the blade and keep the blade out of the water till you lose your balance. When you do, catch yourself by quickly pushing the back of the blade against the water and drawing the blade toward you. You'll have more time to effect your hip snap if you keep the blade moving on the surface. To recover a submerged blade after the brace, just roll your wrist(s) up slightly and bring the blade up forward. Work on smooth technique rather than extreme leans. They come easily when you get the technique.

Start the high brace with your elbows down and wrist(s) rolled back to make the paddle blade horizontal. Reach out, then slowly lean and catch yourself with the power face and use your hips to bring the boat under you. To recover the submerged paddle after your brace, move your upper hand forward and down to bring the blade out toward the back. Practice both braces on both sides, and remember: you are pulling the kayak under you, not pushing yourself onto the kayak.

One final note: a crucial ingredient to the brace is fit. Your brace can make your kayak extremely seaworthy, but you can not brace if your thighs and hips are not snug in the cockpit.

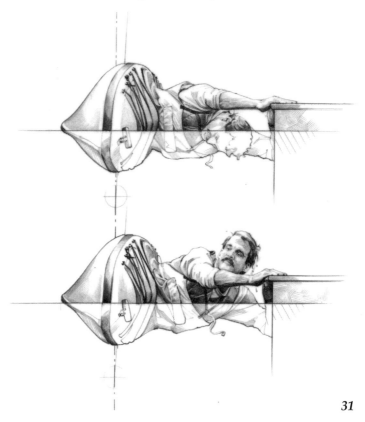

Your head is the last thing to leave the water during the hip snap.

Fight the urge to raise your head and use your arms to pull yourself up.

A Hip Twist by Any Other Name

David Seidman

For years we have been told to use a "hip flick" or "hip snap" to get ourselves back up from a brace or a roll. The phrase has now become a convention in books and instruction courses—an accepted part of the language of kayaking. Unfortunately, the phrase can be misleading.

When knocked over, we use the paddle's bracing motion to support us near the surface. From there, we are told, a deft use of our hip will flick (twist) the boat upright. And technically, that's correct. The rotational force generated by your twisting hips will bring the boat back up. But when done properly, it won't feel like your hips are doing the work. It will feel more like you're lifting the boat with your knee, rather than flicking it around with your rear end.

Your knee lift and hip flick will be more effective if you sit up straight and reduce the pressure on your foot pegs. "Standing" on the pegs and leaning back locks up your anatomy.

Try this. While standing, forcefully rotate your right hip counterclockwise. That's what most of us call a "hip flick." Now do it again, but this time with your right knee raised. Notice how much more powerful it felt? You're still generating the same twisting force with your hips, but now the action is being given extra momentum by your knee. What you've done is a "knee lift."

In a kayak, the knee lift starts by flexing your foot against the foot rest, twisting the hip up on the side to be raised, and driving your knee up against the underside of the deck. At the same time, the hip and buttock on the other side are pushing down. The resultant motion lifts one side of the boat. To get used to the sensation, try alternately lifting one knee and then the other to rock your kayak. It feels like your hips are moving up and down (and they are) but it is actually your knees that are controlling the motion. Remember to sit up straight and don't "stand" on your foot pegs. Leaning back and/or standing on the pegs locks up your anatomy and inhibits the knee/hip action. Try it both ways and you'll see what I mean.

Now practice bringing the boat back up from a near-capsize. Hold on to the dock (or pool side) and pull the kayak over on its side, just to the point of capsize. To bring the boat back up, hold your upper body in place and twist your hips upward at the waist—forcing your knee up against the low side of the boat. The hip's force, imparted by your knee, should rotate the boat upright. Ignore your arms as much as possible; they simply provide a point of balance—the same function your paddle performs in a brace or the last phases of a roll. Your upper body should be completely isolated from the process, with all lifting and righting momentum coming from the lifting of your knee.

Your knees are doing the work for the powerful muscles around your waist. When these muscles are flexed, their momentum, coupled with the driving up of your knee, will bring the kayak up. It's called a hip flick, but it might be more effective if you visualize it as a knee lift.

Staying on Course

Shelley Johnson

Staying on course can be a frustrating experience for the touring kayaker. Watching kayaks "snake wake" through the water is a painful sight, especially if you will agree that the object of the game is to use as little energy as possible to get where you're going. Maintaining your momentum and staying on course are a matter of paying attention and continually reacting to your boat's course and progress.

First, get used to looking ahead at some object by which you can gauge your kayak's position. Too often, novice paddlers fixate on the bow of their boat only

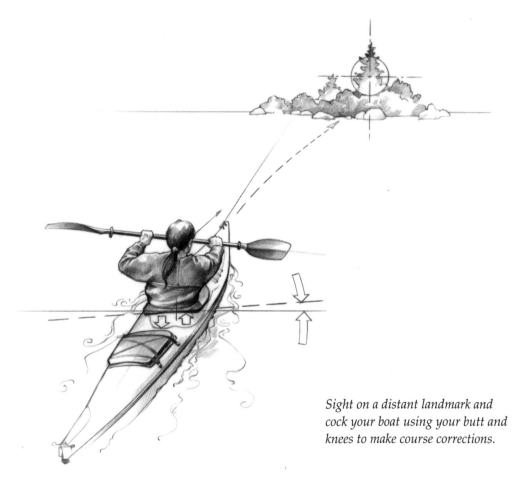

Sight on a distant landmark and cock your boat using your butt and knees to make course corrections.

to look up, startled by how far off course they have wandered. As you become accustomed to your boat and how it feels and moves on the water, you begin to develop a sense of what your boat is doing and how to react to its motion. As your sense of control develops, you'll learn that a course correction is often as simple as a slight weight shift.

If you shift your weight to one side of the boat and continue to paddle forward, you'll notice that the boat will gradually move in the direction away from the weighted, now slightly lower, side of the kayak. In other words, if you shift your weight to your right side, the boat will move to the left as you paddle forward, and vice versa. When you tilt the boat you create unequal pressures on each side of the bow as it moves through the water. With more pressure on the weighted side of the boat, your bow will tend to swing away from that pressure, resulting in a subtle course change. Knowing this and using it to your advantage can save you a lot of energy; you can maintain your forward momentum at the same time you are making course corrections.

To shift your weight, simply lift your buns and knee on one side. Don't throw your weight to the side of the boat or lean out over the water. This weight shift changes the hull shape and waterline length so that the two sides of the boat are no longer equal.

Making these minor course corrections is not the same as executing a turning stroke, which is a far more determined change of course. The weight shift keeps you on course; a turning stroke changes your course, and there is some loss of forward momentum. If shifting your weight is not effective in keeping your boat on course, adjust your forward stroke on the weighted side as well. Reach out farther in more of a sweeping motion, and this will accentuate your course correction while maintaining your forward momentum.

Remember, the idea is to avoid wasting energy. Strokes are continuous and smooth, and your weight shift becomes second nature as you respond to your boat. Like climbing a set of stairs: your body makes a constant appraisal of stair height and depth and you place your foot in the right spot. Dealing with the effects of wind, tidal current, and a weathercocking boat will be far simpler as you tune into your boat's progress and position, and react accordingly.

The Cross-Wind Ferry

Shelley Johnson

River kayakers have long known that setting a proper ferry angle helps to move a boat across a river without being pushed downstream. As sea kayakers, we deal with an analogous situation: we set a ferry angle in relation to the wind strength and direction when making an open crossing. Developing a strategy to deal with a crossing when the wind is abeam will save you a lot of aggravation and energy. We'll call this strategy the cross-wind ferry.

Rather than trying to paddle a straight line across open water with the wind on your beam, think about setting an angle with your bow off the wind so that it points upwind of your final destination (see illustration). Depending on the force of the wind and your strength, your angle will fall somewhere around 45 degrees. By angling your bow, you can "crab" your way across to the far shore in a neat counter-balancing of forward momentum and the force of the cross wind.

Most sea kayaks will tend to turn up into the wind as they make headway. This is known as weathercocking. You can use this to your advantage when setting your ferry angle. Once your angle is set, make sure you maintain a steady momentum and then monitor your angle and position relative to the far shore and final destination. If your bow comes up just off the wind, you'll find yourself paddling in a near headwind and your momentum will slow. If you don't maintain sufficient speed from the start of your crossing, you may find your bow blown off the wind, causing you to skid downwind even more. Constantly monitor your position relative to the wind and reference points on the shore, and make corrections as you go.

Look for a pattern to the wind. Winds are rarely constant, but will gust with moments of calm in between. Take advantage of these little pauses between puffs to make your corrections. Also, turn your boat on the wave crests when the boat ends are out of the water. Shorten your stroke and pick up your cadence when paddling in windy conditions. The quicker cadence will make you feel more stable and enable you to maintain your speed. If you find the going tough, remember to utilize your torso rotation to drive your forward stroke and maximize your power. This is not a time to "lily dip."

Build in a "fudge" factor by planning to hit shore at a point upwind of your final destination. If you begin to tire toward the end of your crossing, you won't be blown past your final destination and be faced with a paddle into a headwind at the very end. If all goes well and you hit shore upwind of your final destination, simply turn and catch a free ride down to the take-out.

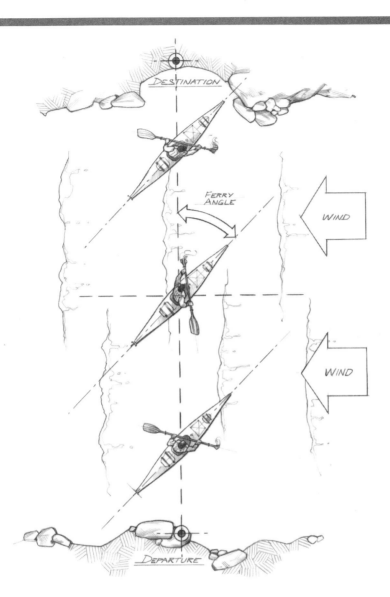

Set an angle that points upwind of your final destination.

As you paddle across, tilt your boat into the wind by lifting your downwind knee. Adjusting the degree of lean will fine-tune your course corrections, as a lean into the wind will counteract the boat's tendency to weathercock. Keep your hips loose as the wind-driven waves pass under your hull, and maintain your paddling cadence.

Recognizing the principles of ferrying and using the wind power to your advantage are valuable strategies for open water crossings. Setting and maintaining a proper ferry angle in relation to the wind and monitoring your progress and position relative to points on shore will minimize the effects of cross winds.

Shoot to Miss

Lee Moyer

Suppose you are on an offshore island and want to go 4 miles to a river mouth on the coastline. You know to head due east and you know there is a strong current along shore. By factoring the direction and distance to the river mouth, the current speed according to your tables, and an estimate of your kayak speed, you plot a course across the channel and take off. But when you arrive at the shore, your target isn't where it's supposed to be. It must be nearby, but do you go north or south along the coast to find it? How far before you turn back to where the other guy said you should have gone first? What could you have done to avoid this mess?

Even with the best documentation of current speed and your rate of travel, you will be lucky to predict your course within half a mile on a 4-mile crossing in strong current. The best solution is to plan to miss from the start so you know which way to go when you reach the coastline.

This is called aiming off, a technique so simple it is often neglected in books and classes on navigation. Yet it is usually the safest and most practical navigation technique for kayaking (and flying small planes), where you are dealing with crude estimates in terms of kayak speed and drift, and it is likely that your navigation will not be very accurate.

In aiming off, it is not important that your navigation be very accurate. The idea works on the underlying principle that you're never really lost. You just aren't there yet.

Let's start out again from the offshore island. By purposely aiming well north of (or "off") the river inlet, you know that once you see the shore (Point A) you'll have to move south to find your objective. In your first attempt you may have arrived at Point B, and you would not know which direction to turn, despite your careful calculations.

In aiming off, you also have the option of overcompensating by paddling "upstream" before you start your crossing, and then paddling back once you see the other side. This appears longer on the chart but in fact may be faster. You need to estimate where protected areas or eddies are. For example, if you are crossing a wide, curved channel to the outside of the bend, there will be strong current along the far shore and less current or maybe a back eddy along the starting shore. It would be easiest to paddle upstream first and then make the crossing and drift downstream to your target.

In areas of strong drift, aiming off will be safer and more accurate than ferrying. You spend less time away from shore and in other boat traffic because the crossing is faster. Also, ferrying doesn't work in drift conditions that are faster than your cruise speed.

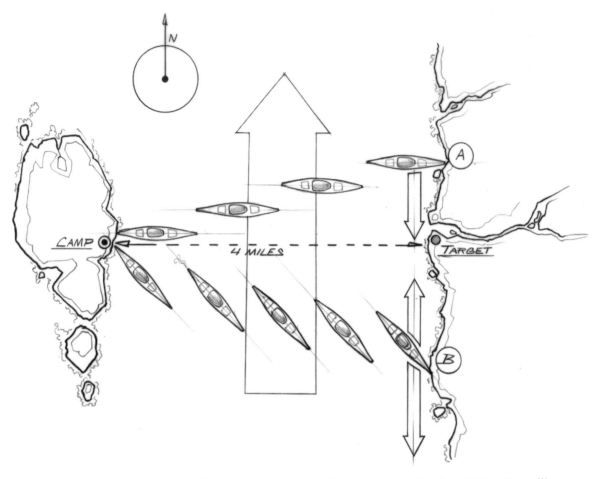

By simply aiming well north of your target, you know that once you see the shore (Point A) you'll have to travel south to find it. If, after carefully computing distance, direction, and cruising and current speeds, you have a near miss (Point B), you won't know which direction to turn, despite your elaborate calculations.

If there is a side wind on a crossing with no current, ignore it (or angle into it sharply for more pleasant paddling) and when you see the other side and not your goal, veer into the wind (or turn downwind if you were overcompensating) and follow the shoreline to your target. You may miss, but you are never in doubt as to which way to go. In the long run you will waste less

energy and time than the paddler who calculates it all out and then doesn't know what to do when he does not arrive at his target.

You will also have a more harmonious group, since there are not diverse opinions about what you should have done. In reality, you probably won't even have a longer crossing, since you can start veering toward your target as soon as you can see shore.

The Blind Crossing

Lee Moyer

A blind crossing is the act of getting to a destination that is obscured by weather. The *reverse azimuth* crossing is a simple way to plot and correct your course when you can't see your destination. The object is to move on a straight line from the launch point to the destination by ferrying across at an angle to offset wind or current. The technique is to estimate a heading and guess how drift will affect it, try it, and correct for error.

First, check the crossing on your map—its length, your direction of travel, and your reverse direction of travel (the direction plus or minus 180 degrees). Guess on the amount of ferry angle necessary to counter the wind or current. Your ferry angle plus the direction of travel equals the heading you should take to allow for drift as you cross.

For example, let's say your desired heading is 218 degrees (A). If you are on course, the reverse direction is 38 degrees, or the direction of your launch site. If the estimated ferry angle is 30 degrees to the right (a reasonable guess to start with), then adjust your heading to 248 degrees.

Now launch into the fog on your estimated heading. Before you lose sight of your launch point, note the reverse direction relative to it (B). Correct your course by whatever angle the launch site is from your reverse direction, and keep paddling on the corrected heading. If you find that the launch site is 5 degrees to the left of your reverse direction, the corrected heading is now 243 degrees (C).

For complete accuracy, you need consistent kayak speed, drift speed, and heading. These variables are difficult to control in bad weather, and wind or current can't be controlled at all. The reverse azimuth technique is a simple way to counter them, using what's behind you to keep you going straight ahead.

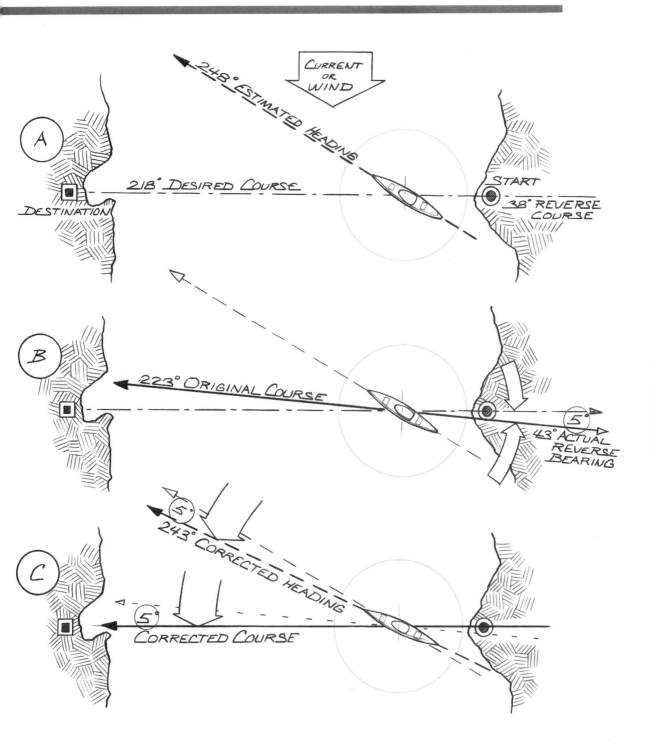

Landing in Surf, Part I

Lee Moyer

Surfing is fun, but compared to other kayaks, a sea kayak is about your last choice for surfing. Since the goal in touring is to get safely to the beach, it's important to know first how to find a landing site where the surf is not so intense, and second, how to react when you get there. Predicting a safe landing beach requires only cursory knowledge of waves and beaches, and a good deal of common sense.

In deep water, waves without wind are easy, smooth rollers. They are fun, safe, and often exciting because of their size. But as these waves approach a beach, they slow down, get closer together, and peak up before finally breaking at a depth only slightly greater than the wave height. Until you've committed to landing, you cannot see the beach over the breaking waves to confirm that the beach is clear of logs, driftwood, rock outcroppings, etc. The romantic notion of casually surfing onto beaches in the wilderness is unrealistic.

How can you be reasonably assured of a safe place to land without firsthand knowledge of the beach? Your chart will tell you a great deal about a beach and the landing conditions there. The chart shows the type of beach (gravel, sand, mud, etc.) and gradient. It also shows shoreline reefs

and rocks that may break up the surf. But more obviously, it shows how a beach is oriented to the predominant swells, and how these swells will react to the land forms as they approach shore.

As the straight waves in deep water move into shallow water, they hit bottom and slow down. When parts of an oncoming wave are traveling in shallower water than others, the straight waves refract, bending until they're almost parallel to the shoreline.

Look at the map of a crescent beach and you can generally predict the way these waves will dissipate their energy there. The straight waves can't make the turn around Point A, a rocky point somewhat parallel to the beach and in deep water. Meanwhile, the waves will attack Point B, which protrudes straight out. Stay away and head for landing site C, in the protected lee of Point A.

Wherever you land, remember to note the predominant direction of the waves as you paddle in the deeper water offshore, since they become parallel with the beach as they approach the surf zone. The surf zone will vary from the long, gradual breaks of spilling waves on a gently sloped beach to the shorter dumping type on a steep beach. Tide height can have a major effect on which it is: Gener-

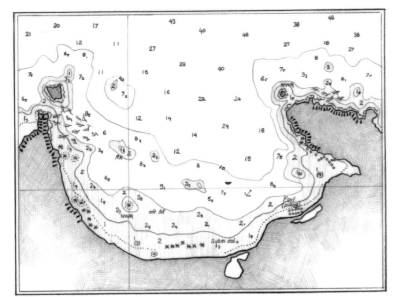

Your chart and a little knowledge of wave refraction will help point you to a safe place to land.

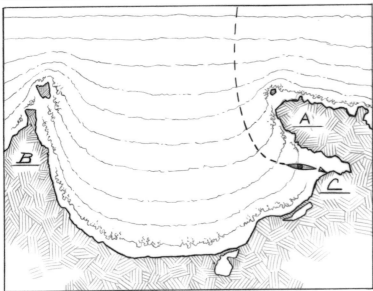

ally, at low tides the surf is the friendly spilling type, and at higher tides, the beach is steeper with a dumping surf. Steeper beaches will have smooth gravel or rocks, so there is a good chance of sliding back down the beach with the receding wave as you land—a good photo opportunity.

Landing in Surf, Part II

Lee Moyer

Surf is like a speedway: lots of speed, power, and spectacular crashes, but in reality, very little danger if you understand how to use it and stay within your limits.

There are two main types of waves that break on the beach: spilling waves and dumping waves. Spilling waves characterize the classic surf beach, where the tops of the waves seem to "spill" down the wave face. They approach the beach in sets, a series of crests and troughs marching toward the beach one after the other.

One way to avoid surfing even large spilling waves is to paddle toward the beach and, as a wave catches you, back-paddle over it, then paddle hard toward the beach again when you're in the low part of the set. With proper timing, you'll stay on the back of each wave as it breaks in front of you. By paddling forward during the lull, you won't be pulled into the wave that's approaching you from behind.

In waves too big to back-paddle over, you can broach and ride the wave in sideways. This isn't true surfing but it is fun, quite safe, and not very difficult. If there is no one to teach you, you can teach this technique to yourself. It requires a reasonably good high brace, the ability to wet-exit with confidence, plus a little courage and a good sense of humor.

First, find a beach that has an onshore wind, big waves (you define big), a gentle slope, and few large obstacles. Since the water will be shallow, wear a helmet, and in colder waters wear a wet suit or dry suit. Bring someone to watch and help you (as in, "I think your paddle is over there"), and don't forget to bring spare dry clothes and have a warm place to recover nearby. Your kayak should be empty and have the maximum amount of flotation. Secure your air bags or sea sock: if you come out of your boat in large surf, inadequate flotation could cost you your kayak.

As you approach the surf from deep water, note where the break starts and keep in mind that it will change with the size of the waves. Back-paddle over the big waves and work your way toward shore during the lulls. Keep your kayak pointed at an angle toward your most comfortable bracing side. When a non-breaking wave comes, stop paddling and lean into it with a combination high brace and draw and let it slide under you.

When a breaking wave comes, do the same high brace but with more lean (remember to keep your elbows low to avoid a dislocated shoulder). The wave will catch your kayak and take it sideways all the way up the beach. You just ride it, leaning hard into the wave and high bracing. Your high brace into the wave will not sink because of the green water sliding under the kayak and out to sea as the white water rolls in over it. This local current differential makes even a marginal

The controlled broach: the spilling breaker will turn your boat sideways. Lean into the wave on your high brace and ride sideways up the beach.

high brace bomb-proof if you just have faith and lean into it enough.

Landing in dumping surf is different. In fact, on a very steep beach, it may not be possible. Unlike spilling surf, dumping waves curl and break onto little or no water, just a steep, rocky beach that offers no soft landing for a broached kayak or one surfing down the face of a dumping wave. Riding a dumping wave means you will probably hit bottom, so lean forward. If a wave breaks on you as you are upside down, you can hit bottom hard on your back.

Due to the steepness of the beach, you can get relatively close to the beach to scout the wave action. In a couple minute cycle, you'll notice that the waves progress from small to large and back again. Count the waves to note about how many are in a cycle. Timing is critical. Position yourself outside the break zone and wait for the large wave part of the set, so you end up well up the beach when you land. Let a couple go by, then pick one. Let it pass

under you and then sprint for shore behind it. The result should be an easy ride well up the beach on the back of the wave. When the wave runs out, hold yourself in position until you are grounded, then get out and very quickly pull your kayak far up the beach.

If you catch the wave late and the wave is receding as you approach the beach, you can be swept sideways and back out. High brace and lean into the next breaking wave and try to ride it up the beach. You will get wet as it dumps on you, but a strong lean and brace may fool the spectators into thinking you know what you are doing as you wash sideways back up the beach. You may have to catch yourself with the paddle and scramble out to continue what is now more of a salvage operation than a surf landing. If you are swimming, try to hang onto your kayak but do not get shoreward of it where the waves are breaking or it will be swept over you. Even if you are only wading and dragging it behind you up the beach, watch out.

45

How to Punch Through Surf

David Seidman

The first rule for getting out through the surf safely is to be patient. Take your time to look for patterns in the surf. You'll soon see that the larger waves come in sets—a definable pattern. To decipher this pattern you may be able to count the waves or time the period between them. Neither system is absolutely accurate. Your best bet is to remember how the largest waves look, and what comes before them. Try to envision a window of opportunity. You want to be nearing the surf line after the largest wave of a set has spent itself. Be patient and wait.

Try to avoid surf more than 6 feet high. You can judge heights by standing at the water's edge. If the top of a breaking wave extends over the horizon line, it is higher than your eye level (say, 5½ feet). Do the same for smaller waves by standing on your knees (about 4 feet) or seated (about 2½ feet).

After launching, paddle toward the surf zone with short, brisk strokes so you

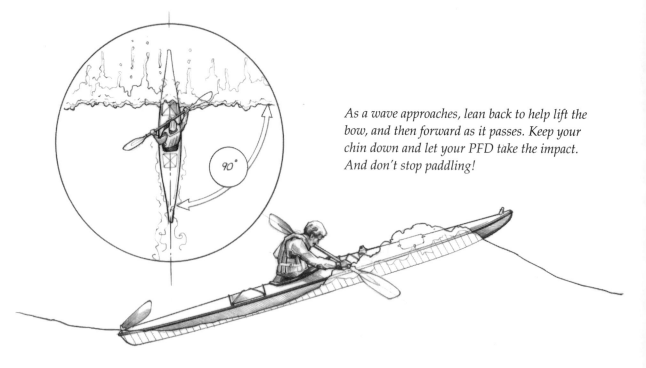

As a wave approaches, lean back to help lift the bow, and then forward as it passes. Keep your chin down and let your PFD take the impact. And don't stop paddling!

can react fast to balance or alter direction. Stay at right angles to the waves, holding back or sprinting to miss the worst of it. If you are lucky, you'll have to push through only the soup (white water) or over a swell. As a wave approaches, lean back to help lift the bow, and then forward as it passes, all the time aggressively paddling to claw your way over. You'll do it if you just keep paddling.

When you are not so lucky, and it looks like a small wave (less than three feet) might break on you, keep your head down and chin buried in your PFD. Time your strokes so that when the wave hits the bow, a blade will be entering the solid part of the wave. As the wave reaches you, pull yourself through and let your PFD take the impact. Do not stop paddling or hold the paddle over your head with the idea that the wave will pass around you. It will, but it will also wash you backwards or smash the paddle shaft rudely back into you. Paddle through with force. If the wave is steep, you'll come flying out the back like a Polaris missile.

If you're about to be pounded by a towering monster, dig in and paddle hard—the plan is to build up maximum momentum so you will punch right through it. Keep your weight forward and your head down, so the water will have less to grab. It is crucial that you avoid being hit in the upper body by the full force of the wave; this can drive you back or (worse) over and back. Paddle on no matter what. As you emerge from the wave's back, congratulate yourself, take a deep breath, and beat a hasty path out of the surf line. Keep up a steady pace until you are farther out than you would think necessary; otherwise, a large set may come through, taking you by surprise.

Readiness Builds Confidence: Know Your Gear

Shelley Johnson

Part of the appeal of sea kayaking is that it offers self-sufficiency and simplicity: just you, your boat, and the seascape. But that same self-sufficiency places the burden of being prepared on every sea kayaker, whether on an easy afternoon paddle or a ten-day expedition.

Beyond the obvious essentials of a boat with proper flotation, paddle, and PFD, a plethora of gear is available to keep you prepared for the expected as well as the unexpected. There is gear to keep you found, protected from the elements, visible, and self-sufficient. But it is not enough to simply purchase gear. You need to know when and how to use it, where to store it, and how to maintain it.

Safety gear and essential equipment need to be stored where they are readily accessible. Know exactly where you've stored specific items and be consistent about where you put them, on or in the boat. Don't just throw everything into a dry bag. Keep your essentials compartmentalized: put the signaling devices together, spare clothes in a separate dry bag, and boat repair materials separated from everything else. An emergency isn't the time to have to remember if the pliers for a rudder repair are at the bottom of the clothes bag, or whether your flares are in the chart case or the first-aid kit.

Getting all of your safety gear properly stored and accessible requires planning and ingenuity, and each boat seems to dictate its own configuration. Store gear under your foredeck as long as it doesn't impede a wet exit; otherwise, it should be clipped or tethered to the boat. Add deck rigging to hold a spare paddle on the rear deck, or gear eyes to attach gear to the deck or behind the seat. Consider Velcro attachments for gear stored inside the cockpit.

Think about what you might need to grab from your boat in the event of a capsize and wet exit. Could you carry some smaller flares on your PFD or in a spray-skirt pocket? How about attaching a whistle to your PFD zipper tab and a strobe high on your shoulder, where it can be seen even if you're bobbing in the water? Can you easily get to your bilge pump and paddle float if you need to do a re-entry, or is all your safety gear bobbing around like a nautical yard sale because it wasn't properly stowed?

Run through the safety scenarios in your mind and then practice them on and in the water. Make sure you can get your paddle float from underneath the deck rigging with one hand while you're in the water alongside your boat. Ensure that your tow line is easily deployed and can be quickly detached when needed. Too often, items are stuffed behind a seat or buried underneath other gear on the deck, preventing easy access. Simply remembering to bring safety gear is not sufficient; you must be able to get to it and use it properly in real conditions. Practice this. Cold water and wind can add unforeseen wrinkles to accessing equipment and using it, so practice in these conditions.

Maintenance is important, too. Check your gear for corrosion, punctures, expiration dates, if applicable, or anything else that might affect performance. Water and sun are tough on equipment; without proper maintenance, waterproof seals can crack and metal closures can become unusable.

How you pack, store, and maintain your safety gear is all part of your overall strategy as a sea kayaker. As you grow more confident in your paddling skills, you should also grow more confident in your safety gear and its use. Because the reward of being prepared is the freedom to paddle where and when you choose and knowing that you can take care of yourself.

Your own boat may call for a different set-up.

Stuff It!

Lee Moyer

How a sea kayak handles depends largely on how the load is balanced or "trimmed" fore to aft. Some kayaks handle very well when empty yet change their personalities when loaded. Adverse trim effects due to loading or design deficiencies can be overcome with a rudder. But if the rudder is working hard, it is producing considerable drag. It's better to trim the kayak properly.

Proper trim is not obvious. Setting a kayak on the floor and marking each end for a reference line will not necessarily produce an accurate, level trim line. Eyeballing the deck profile also is misleading, since some kayaks are styled to have rakish appearance, others to have a minimum end profile. If one assumes the kayak is properly balanced on the water when empty, the best way to establish a level ref-

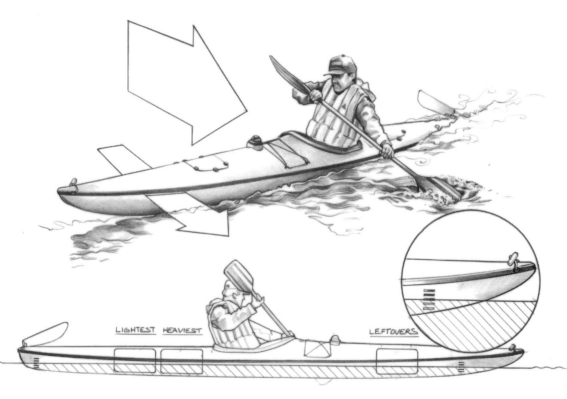

LIGHTEST HEAVIEST   LEFTOVERS

erence trim line is to mark the actual waterline while the paddler sits in the kayak in calm water. Then, by marking and labelling increments above the noted waterline, it is easy to see if the loaded kayak is still balanced.

Compared to level trim, bow-heavy trim produces a lower bow and higher stern. At the bow, this reduces the area exposed to the wind and increases the keel effect below the waterline. At the stern, the effect is just the opposite. As you paddle forward into a cross wind, the wind will blow the stern downwind while the bow stays securely anchored by its deeply entrenched keel. A bow-heavy kayak thus turns into the wind. Interestingly, a bow-heavy kayak with no hull speed will drift sideways to the wind, and at high hull speeds, the cross wind has less effect. The problem is most noticeable just below cruise speed. Bow-heavy trim also causes strong oversteer and makes control difficult even in good conditions.

Due to convenience and ignorance, most kayaks are paddled stern-heavy. Stern-heavy trim makes the kayak track very well in calm water, run easily with waves and surf, and resist pointing into the wind. Unless the weather gets bad, paddlers in stern-heavy kayaks won't know any better and assume they are properly trimmed. When the wind kicks up, you can identify these paddlers by their colorful vocabulary and desperate backstrokes as their kayaks seem determined to run downwind into a problem.

One way to ensure a well-balanced load is to divide all the cargo into three equal-sized piles, with the lightest stuff in one pile, the heaviest in another, and the leftovers in the third. Load the leftovers (about a third of the total) into the bow, the lightest pile into the stern toward the end of the kayak, and the heaviest last into the stern, close to the center of the kayak. You'll modify this system as experience shows how the kayak handles and whether you really have time to unload most of the gear to get to the toilet paper.

It's best to establish a consistent loading pattern so the kayak is always predictable, rather than arranging the load for the expected conditions. They change faster than the paddler can rearrange his gear for optimum trim.

Emptying a Kayak

Lee Moyer

While tipovers are rare in touring, knowing how to aid a paddler in the water should one occur is an important skill, one you should practice regularly.

There are two parts to performing a rescue: getting the water out of the kayak and getting the victim back into the kayak. Which comes first—and whether you choose to pump or dump the water from the kayak—depends on the conditions, the rescue technique, and equipment involved.

If the kayak does not have a bulkhead near the cockpit, it will probably have to be pumped out. Pumping water from a flooded kayak can take half an hour if the kayak has minimal flotation and the victim pumps alone, or only a few minutes if the kayak has good flotation and the victim has helpers to stabilize the kayak and pump. It's generally best to first help the victim stabilize and re-enter the kayak using a secure paddle float or your kayak as a brace before beginning to pump. In any but the most benign conditions, the victim must re-attach his sprayskirt to avoid taking more water.

If the kayak can be dumped out quickly, empty it first and then help the victim re-enter. It is probably better to leave the paddler in the water an extra few minutes so you can put him into a dry, empty kayak than to put him into a partly flooded, unstable kayak and then take fifteen to thirty minutes to pump out the water, assuming all goes well.

With assistance, water can be quickly dumped from the kayak without having to lift the boat from the water, if the kayak has a bulkhead at the back of the cockpit. The paddler in the water swims to the stern and turns the flooded kayak upside down to trap as much air in the cockpit as possible. The rescuer then moves his kayak perpendicular to the victim's. Pushing down on the stern of the kayak, the victim then lifts himself out of the water as he supports himself over the stern on stiff arms. He also controls the kayak to keep it from flipping upright. The rescuer uses one hand to lift the bow while the victim rotates the kayak slightly to break the seal at the cockpit and allow the water to flow out. The trick is to not let the kayak turn upright until it's empty.

Designs with adequate stern flotation can be emptied unassisted if the victim is heavy enough, the kayak is empty of gear, and conditions are calm. This is not a realistic rescue situation, but it is a good drill.

Dumping water from a kayak with no bulkhead requires a more elaborate system, such as the "HI" rescue. The HI rescue requires two rescuers and is unreliable in rough conditions. It is stressful to both kayakers and gear because the partially flooded kayak has to be lifted completely

The rescuer uses one hand to lift the bow while the person in the water rotates the kayak slightly to break the seal at the cockpit and allow the water to flow out.

out of the water. The HI rescue is described more extensively in other literature, but in essence, tow rescuers get their kayaks side-by-side and place their paddles across both cockpits in front of them and, with the assistance of the victim, lift the bow of the victim's upside-down kayak and draw the kayak up between them until the cockpit is over the paddles. They rock the kayak to empty water, right it when empty, and slide the boat back into the water where the victim re-enters with the assistance of the rescuers.

Of course, a boat with flotation can't accept as much water as one without. An airbag in each end is one way to displace water, but a stern bulkhead (just behind the seat) is a major improvement because you can turn the boat over and let the water spill out through the cockpit, no pump required. A bow bulkhead is better than a bow float bag, but it is not as significant as the stern bulkhead. The closer the bulkheads are to the paddler, the better the flotation.

The ultimate flotation is a sea sock or pod. A sea sock is a waterproof nylon bag that seals at the cockpit. The sock encloses you in the kayak so the only place for water is where your body is. While sea socks can be added to any kayak, pods are usually built in to the kayak hull. Both eliminate useful space around the seat for your lunch, camera, rain gear, fishing gear, etc.

Rigging for Paddle-Float Rescue

Lee Moyer

If you are out of your sea kayak and without assistance, one of the best tools for self-rescue is a paddle float. You attach the float, usually inflatable, to the paddle and then secure the paddle to the kayak, forming an outrigger. This stabilizes the boat so you can re-enter, attach your sprayskirt, pump out the water, retrieve your paddle, stow the float, and continue. Much has been written about the actual re-entry drill, but the key to the paddle-float rescue is in how you secure the paddle to the kayak. The rigging system must be sound and simple to be effective in adverse con-

To attach the paddle, release the line from the farthest jam cleat and unhook the center loop of the line from the tee cleats. Lay your paddle across the kayak aft of the tee cleats, hook the loop back under the tee cleats, and cinch up the slack at the near jam cleat.

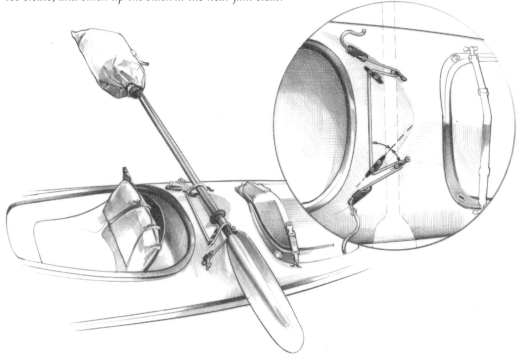

ditions. The most common is a web of shockcords on a flat rear deck. This is adequate, but sometimes the shockcords are just too wimpy.

One rigging system that works well uses a pair of tee cleats, a pair of jam cleats, and a pair of eyestraps placed a few inches behind the cockpit. A 1/4-inch nylon line runs from one jam cleat aft through the eyestrap, forward around the tee cleat, then across the kayak and around the other tee cleat, aft through the eyestrap, and forward to the jam cleat. Figure-8 knots in the ends of the line will keep it permanently attached to the kayak.

Details of the layout will vary with the model of kayak, but several considerations are important. Be sure to leave enough room between the paddle-shaft placement and the cockpit coaming so you can put on your sprayskirt before you release the paddle. Try to keep the eyestraps and tee cleats as close to the edge of the kayak as possible and place them such that the paddle shaft will nest between them. The axis of the tee cleats and eyestraps should bisect the angle formed by the rope. The jam cleats should be located where they will not accidentally catch other lines.

To attach the paddle, release the line from the farthest jam cleat and unhook the center loop of the line from the tee cleats. Lay your paddle across the kayak aft of the tee cleats, hook the loop back under the tee cleats, and cinch up the slack at the near jam cleat. There is no threading or tying involved, and you can rig the system as you lay across the back of the kayak. When you're in the cockpit, simply release either jam cleat and pull the paddle forward to remove it from the rigging. In the stowed position, the line serves as a good place to store your paddle float.

Keeping a Weather Eye Out

Shelley Johnson

Since even the most powerful supercomputers are unable to accurately predict weather on a local scale, people often shrug and accept what comes. For kayakers, this approach is foolhardy.

Preparing for the weather starts long before you pack your gear and load your boat. You need to monitor both weather reports for your area and national weather maps to ascertain developing patterns that could affect your paddling. Small weather radios, Internet weather sites, and local TV weather reports all make it easy to pick up current weather information.

Get familiar with weather terminology and understand what it means. *Chapman Piloting* is an excellent source of weather definitions and explanations for small boaters. For instance, know that wind directions are reported as blowing *from* (SE, NW, W, etc.) or blowing *to* (offshore, onshore). Knowing the wind direction of offshore breezes for your paddling area is critical. You might be comfortable paddling in a 15- to 20-knot wind, but not if it is blowing offshore. This knowledge is essential for trip planning, even for an afternoon paddle.

Since wind is such a critical factor for sea kayakers, get in the habit of observing water and land features at different wind velocities. Watch how the surface of the water can change from ripples to whitecaps to streaks, or how trees sway as the wind velocity changes. A handy reference for relating wind velocity to water conditions is called the Beaufort scale. Get a copy and relate it to what you observe in your own paddling area. Particular weather conditions or wind directions should put you on alert. Getting caught on open water as a cold front moves through can be dangerous; winds may shift and increase dramatically. However, the other side of a cold front can be delightful paddling, so timing is everything. Know that an offshore breeze is a condition to be taken seriously. Be aware of those wind directions whose effects are magnified by such topographical features as narrow channels, headlands, shoals, and the like.

Review the relationship between your tides and the forecast wind direction. If a strong tidal flow is opposed by a strong wind, you can expect chop and steepening waves. In a constricted area such as a river mouth, this can be dangerous. By listening to weather reports and relating them to the chart of your paddling area, you can avoid this situation.

Weather changes rapidly, and wind direction may shift over the course of a day. Local sea breezes may develop during the afternoon, or weather fronts moving into an area may cause a significant change in the wind's direction and velocity. Watch cloud movements and formations; they are enormously useful in predicting the local weather pattern. Observe how fast they are moving. Look for ragged edges on clouds or the towering anvil shape of a cumulonimbus cloud, or thunderhead, which suggests violent forces aloft and instability.

If you're planning a multi-day excursion, look for cloud patterns that signal changes in the weather: high wispy clouds that lower and gradually thicken, for example, or clearly defined front lines. Compare your observations to the weather reports to test your predictions.

Knowing weather is essential for any boater.

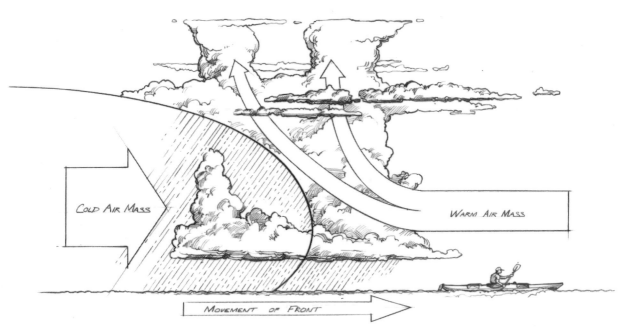

COLD AIR MASS

WARM AIR MASS

MOVEMENT OF FRONT

Learn to recognize the cloud patterns. Here's the classic cold front scenario.

In Search of Dolphins

Dave Harrison

One of my friends, trying to explain sea kayaking's surge in popularity, said that he thought people were really just fascinated by the gadgetry associated with the sport. He meant, of course, hardware like bilge pumps, deck compasses, sail rigs, high-tech hatch covers, and paddle floats. But in the realm of gizmos, nothing beats Chart No. 1 on a cost-benefit basis.

The National Oceanic and Atmospheric Administration (NOAA) prepares the charts used for coastal navigation by sailors and kayakers alike. At a chart store, these charts run you $10 to $15. For the uninitiated, a good part of that value is lost in what appear to be squiggles, obscure abbreviations, icons, and assorted hieroglyphics. Fortunately, for the incredibly low price of $2.50, there is a publication called Chart No. 1—also produced by the NOAA and available at any chart store. This chart can prove to be the mariner's Rosetta stone for decoding all that gibberish.

Poring over the 1:80,000 chart for the coastal waters of Washington State's Olympic Peninsula, you see the notations "dols" and "dol." These mean nothing to many, but after working through the list of abbreviations and weaving back through the cross-references, you discover the notations mean "dolphins." "How nice of NOAA to clue us in on the whereabouts of our local marine life!"—we think, until checking a lit-

tle further and realizing that "dolphin" is synonymous with "mooring buoy."

So Chart No. 1 does assume some elementary knowledge of nautical terms, but don't let that deter you if you are new to this game. And if you want to get good at the sea kayaking game, this chart is invaluable.

Much of what passes for navigation in the world of sea kayaking is really piloting, finding your way by means of natural landmarks or man-made features, like lights, buoys, and channel markers. Pay attention to those aids. Cruising along, it's easy to incorrectly count headlands and misread a coastal contour. A light is a positive identification.

Most importantly, you should familiarize yourself with navigational danger symbols: rocks and rocky areas, tide rips, breakers, and kelp or seaweed beds. When it's time to find a beach for camping, you will want to recognize and decipher the squiggles, symbols, and color-shadings that suggest good landing areas. Cryptic notations like "S" (sand), "G" (gravel), or "Cb" (cobbles) detail the composition of shore and foreshore. There are 16 different notations in all, truly more than you need to know.

In tidal current areas, you had better heed those little arrows, some with feathers and some without. The feathered arrow—carrying a maximum current